Origins

An Immigrant's Journey in America

Thy Nguyen

NEW DEGREE PRESS
COPYRIGHT © 2020 THY NGUYEN
All rights reserved.

ORIGINS
An Immigrant's Journey in America

ISBN   978-1-64137-414-9 *Paperback*
           978-1-64137-415-6 *Kindle Ebook*
           978-1-64137-416-3 *Ebook*

Origins

Contents

NOTE FROM THE AUTHOR 7

INTRODUCTION.	JOURNEY TO AMERICA AND OVERVIEW	13
Chapter 1.	Moving to America	15
Chapter 2.	High School and the In-Between	17
Chapter 3.	Overview	21

PART 1.	INITIAL IDENTITY ANXIETIES	25
Chapter 4.	Neither Here nor There	27
Chapter 5.	Shame, Shame, Shame	31
Chapter 6.	Microaggressions	39

PART 2.	WHAT IN THE WORLD IS HAPPENING TO US?	47
Chapter 7.	In the Media	49
Chapter 8.	Asian-American Underrepresentation in Hollywood	53
Chapter 9.	Get Me Out of This Box	69
Chapter 10.	Mistreatment	77

PART 3.	ACCEPTANCE AND RESOLUTION	81
Chapter 11.	Citizenship Oath Swearing Ceremony	83
Chapter 12.	Rise Up	87
Chapter 13.	Know Your Worth	91
Chapter 14.	Resolution	105

Note from the Author

―――

"Can you help me with my Chinese homework?" the boy with the glasses and scruffy hair asked me.

Matt... was it? Or was it Jack? I was the new student at Lanier Middle School who had just moved from Saigon, Vietnam, to Houston, Texas, so I was still trying to remember everyone's names. My classmates and I were waiting outside the English classroom between fourth and fifth period, all in one neatly formed yet rowdy line.

I looked up at Matt inquisitively and with a sheepish smile, replied, "No, sorry...?"

He seemed surprised. He definitely assumed that I could speak Chinese. I have to say that I was a bit surprised at his surprise, since as the new student, I had just introduced myself in class last week as Vietnamese. What was up with that? Am I supposed to know Chinese? Should I... go learn it? I wonder... are all Asians in America presumed to be Chinese? I let my thoughts trail until my curiosities were interrupted by the loud "RIIING!" of the bell. With a jolt, I marched along with the rest of my classmates in a single file line into the classroom. What did America have in store for me?

My name is Thy Nguyen [pronounced Tea Win], or Nguyễn Đan Thy, and I am sharing the story of the first unintentional microaggression I experienced in the United States. It was my second week at Lanier Middle School. I was still trying to wrap my head around the long, loopy highways, the magnificent drive-thrus at McDonald's, the late 8:30 p.m. sunsets, the abundance of people walking their dogs outside, the cafeteria lunch line . . . everything was new to me. With this new life came many new realizations. One of the first was that I was different—from the color of my skin, to the shape of my eyes, to my childhood and upbringing in Vietnam.

Since moving to America, I have experienced certain feelings of alienation as I navigated my way through life in a new country. One of the first events that added to my alienation was Halloween. In America, Halloween was a whole event— grandiose, exhilarating, and necessary. Everybody dressed up and went trick-or-treating. I loved the atmosphere around Halloween time. Students bustled in the hallways and had passionate debates about what costume to wear and the best neighborhoods for trick-or-treating. On my first American Halloween night, I realized that Halloween was not as easy as I thought it would be. I went through countless lists of potential characters that I could dress up as, but I quickly realized that all my favorite characters were . . . well, white.

As an Asian person, I felt awkward about dressing up as a white character. I did not have the right hair—that was the biggest part. I did not have the right eyes. I did not know what to do. I was a bit disappointed upon realizing that I was not the same as my favorite characters growing up. I eventually gave up on trying to be a cool character and settled for dressing up as a black cat. I know, lame. But it was still a fun and memorable first American Halloween. Over the years, I learned to care less about whether my hair color or eye shape was the same as my character on Halloween. *Screw it*, I said, and I just went for it. This year, for Halloween, I dressed up as Barbie. The Barbie in all pink, with a head full of blonde hair, and yes, who is white. I dressed up in all pink and rocked my dark brown hair with a clip-on pink hair streak that I bought from Party City. I was a *great* Barbie.

Halloween is only one of the numerous alienations I have experienced in America. Over the years, I have been the target of countless racial microaggressions and ignorance. During my teenage years, it was difficult to feel fully comfortable with my identity as an Asian immigrant girl in Texas. For one, I realized how I was underrepresented in the media, and it was disheartening. I could never fully identify with my favorite characters because, racially, we were different. I also faced many racial microaggressions or genuine ignorance, such as backhanded comments telling me I am very "pretty ... for an Asian." I mean, are Asians supposed to be ugly?

People were, and still are, ignorant. In social media comments, I have seen some extremely appalling things. One time, someone commented on an Asian comedian's post and said, "An example of why we shouldn't have stopped at Nagasaki." I was horrified to see someone make such a violently hateful and racist comment. Furthermore, generalizing identification among all Asians undermines diverse cultural identity and individuality. Another time, an Asian girl posted a video of her drawing, and a comment read, "She's really suppose [sic] to be doing math." Are Asians not allowed to have different interests? Stereotypes have targeted people of every situation and background for centuries, but it is important to celebrate what separates one human from another. Putting people into one box diminishes their value; everyone deserves to be seen for who they truly are.

Even though my experiences may not be the most dramatic or life-altering, they make up the true story of me. In recent years, Asian representation in the United States has grown significantly. More and more, we are finally getting a voice. I want to add my piece to the Asian-American narrative and do the community justice through my voice. In addition to writing this book, I want to try my best to be a social justice ally for Asian-Americans. I want to help little by little, even if some efforts are more minor than others.

One of the projects I currently work on at Babson College is the Babson Vietnamese Student Association (BVSA). When I first got to school, I realized there was no solid community for Vietnamese students. So, I founded the BVSA, which aims to create an inclusive community for Vietnamese students, educate general Babson students on Vietnamese culture, and push people to be more open-minded and embrace diversity. The BVSA's mission is to foster inclusivity, not only for Vietnamese students, but also for students who do not know much about the culture. By learning about the struggles and experiences of Asian-Americans, we can inspire others to embrace diversity, culture, and differences. I have always loved writing and have regularly written poems to process my thoughts and feelings, so I was naturally drawn to writing as the medium to voice my story. In addition to poetry, I have always been drawn to writing academic essays in class on Asian-American culture, stereotypes, and struggles.

Origins is the story of my eight-year journey of growth and acceptance as an Asian girl in America. I started off as a girl who was insecure about her race—a girl with many anxieties and feelings of alienation. I have since grown to accept myself and become more comfortable in my own skin. *Origins* is about my personal growth from an anxious girl, confused and at times even ashamedof my own identity, to a proud Asian woman.

This book is separated into three main parts. Prior to the main narrative, the brief introduction details my initial journey to America and includes an overview of the book. The first part consists of stories from the past and anxieties from which I have grown and moved on. The second part contains stories of what other Asian-Americans, including friends and loved ones, are experiencing in the United States. The third part is about my resolution and acceptance of identity. Through short stories, essays, and poems, I share my own and others' experiences with racial prejudice and ignorance in the United States.

Other topics include Asian under-representation, racial microaggressions, feelings of alienation, racial violence, and discrimination. There is a lot to unpack, but I believe these issues can be solved with empathy and an appreciation for individuality. If we all learn to understand one another, we would be able to make peace more easily. I hope to be a voice that makes you feel less alone or tell an eye-opening story for those interested in learning more. For now, enjoy reading!

Introduction
Journey to America and Overview

Chapter 1

Moving to America

In America, the beads of sweat I was used to during Vietnam's steamy 100-degree winters were replaced by goosebumps during the brisk winter season. Busy and chaotic streets filled with motorcycles were replaced with spacious roads and cars that zoomed like lightning. On every corner, local street food vendor carts were replaced with strip malls and grandiose drive-thrus at fast-food restaurants. It was like being plucked out of one life and then being swiftly thrown into another. That is what moving here felt like.

I remember when my parents told me I was going to be moving halfway across the world. I received the news during the summer between seventh and eighth grade. I was sitting at my kitchen counter, the smell of toast wafting through the air and the sound of my brothers yelling at each other ringing in my ears. My mom walked into the kitchen in her bright pink yoga clothes and announced, "We're moving to America!" Naturally, I thought she was joking since it was too abrupt to be true. We had visited relatives in America before, but my parents had never told me and my siblings anything about a permanent stay. When she proceeded to give me the details of our plane flight and of the middle schools that we would tour, however, I realized she was serious, and my laughter came to a halt.

Confused and incredulous, I demanded that she explain what exactly was going on, but all she could say was, "We're moving there for you kids, for a better life."

I asked her what that even meant. "Our lives are perfectly fine here!" I yelled.

I was livid. Did she really expect me to drop everything and leave without a sufficient explanation? The next hour consisted of me arguing with her, demanding some sort of explanation, and bawling my eyes out, but the explanation never came. I had to leave, no questions asked. That night, I begrudgingly packed up all my favorite things and some clothes and angrily threw them into my purple suitcase. Within a week, we took the first flight out to Houston, Texas. Only eight years later did my mom reveal that "we moved for economic stability."

Chapter 2

High School and the In-Between

After being in America for three years, I was in my junior year of high school at Awty International School. At this point in time, my name was Tie, Thigh, or occasionally mixed up with the names of my other Asian classmates like Chan Mye or Jessica, but generally I was known as Thy (pronounced "Tea," like the drink). I did not mind the name confusion, really. My parents did it all the time to American names, especially with friends who came over to our house.

One time, my mom asked, "Is Annabel coming over again this weekend?"

I laughed and stressed to her, "No! Carrie, not Annabel!"

I completely understood why people would confuse two ethnically similar names. Honestly, even I did it sometimes. I remember when I read *American Born Chinese* in English class my junior year. Everyone mixed up the two Chinese protagonists' names, Jin Yang and Wei Chen, but I mixed up Amelia and Suzy, the two American names. We were discussing the characters one time in class and I accidentally said Amelia instead of Suzy, confused everyone, then turned beet red for a good ten minutes.

I liked my high school because it was the closest substitute for the international schools that I attended back in Vietnam. For the most part, people were open minded, friendly, and unique. What I loved most, though, was that students there came from all around the world. Exchanging travel stories, quirks, and just about anything non-American was the highlight of my experience at Awty International School. Walking into school on Lunar New Year and seeing flashes of red and gold everywhere was a heart-warming reminder of Vietnam. However, being the only Vietnamese immigrant at the school did get lonely sometimes. Unlike other European or Asian students, I was not able to talk to anyone in my native language. Just for once, I wanted to be the one chattering secretively to my friend in the hallway in my mother tongue instead of the Spanish or Dutch speakers.

This was the point in time when I first started to feel an identity crisis and started to question the meaning of "home." High school in America made me navigate new relationships, thoughts, and emotions through an American lens, which made me feel more and more American as the years passed. This also made me drift further away from my Vietnamese roots, casting me in the odd area of the in-between. I was not yet fully American, but I also felt unsettled with claiming to be Vietnamese. My Vietnamese accent, my manners, and my clothes were all wrong.

I read a poem in English class that year about a girl who felt like she was sliding past family members like wet cornstarch, unable to attach to anything because of her language barrier. I too felt like the wet cornstarch that could not truly feel like I could attach to any nationality because of the way I pronounced things and the way I looked. I felt like I could not claim neither my Vietnamese identity nor an American one.

Chapter 3

Overview

Two Homes, Two Hearts

If you ask me, *Where is home for you?*
I'm going to tell you that I have two.
Vietnam and the United States,
those are the places that make my heart race.

Moving countries made me struggle immensely
with my ever-changing identity,
I felt a connection with two different homes
which made my personality hard to own.

I felt I was stuck in a corridor,
standing on neither the ceiling nor floor.
Stuck in a constant state of in-between
it really made me a confused teen.

How can one be distant yet connected at the same time?
I still can't tell the difference between a nickel and a dime!
I like using Celsius over Fahrenheit
It makes more sense, it sounds more right.

Yet the more years I spend away from Vietnam
I feel like a foreigner, a fake, a scam.
The waiters at restaurants speak to me in English
Can't you tell that I can speak your language?

My childhood home is getting further away
which keeps my family in constant dismay
I have lost my identity, my language, my culture—
like I have forgotten nature, overcome by nurture.

O say can you see,
America is also the home for me!
But since freedom of speech is at my liberty,
I have to admit sometimes I feel so lonely.

Age-old traditions like Thanksgiving and the Fourth
of July,
haven't been etched in me—we're still different, them and I.
Flying the red, white, and blue,
there are things I have yet to immerse into.

Vietnam is the place where I was born,
but America is the place where I was raised.
My core personality traits are a jarring combination
that sometimes makes me feel like an abomination.

Like a two-headed dragon,
or a beast with two hearts.
Never able to jump on the bandwagon,
but that actually just might be the best part.

Switching languages like I'm switching gears,
my differences make me wise beyond my years.
Vietnamese traditions and manners? Got all those,
American values and ideals? I'm a pro!

Sensitivity and grace toward different backgrounds,
I try to be open, since I'm not nation bound.
What I have is unique,
there is nothing I'd tweak—

Now I realize the beauty

in my dual nationality.
I see the world through many lenses,
different views and many senses.

Part 1
Initial Identity Anxieties

Chapter 4

Neither Here nor There

———

Every year since I left Vietnam in eighth grade, I have gone back and visited during summer vacation. In the first few years that I went back and visited, I was always sad to leave. However, as the years passed, I felt myself drifting further and further away from the place where I had spent my childhood days. For a while, the state of non-belonging had taken over and made me feel hopeless. I felt like I could not fit in. I was also ashamed that even after twelve years of living in Vietnam, I was such a foreigner. This disconnect that once began as a small tug in the back of my neck, a sort of ache or an itch, became a web slowly spreading to every crevice of my body. This disconnect made me feel like I was drifting between worlds, neither here nor there.

I am seventeen now, and this summer, I flew back to Vietnam again. When I was at the airport gate waiting for my flight, there was a Vietnamese couple in a heated argument with a flight attendant at the gate. They were angrily complaining that they could not be seated next to each other. I could not hear their conversation too clearly but was pulled in by their familiarity. They had thick Vietnamese accents, and had a certain special fierceness to them that I often see in Vietnamese people. The flight attendant told them that she would "be right back," and the couple started arguing among themselves in Vietnamese. For some reason, just hearing the language made me feel safe and comforted and made me want to listen to their whole conversation. My connection with them felt almost familial. I could tell that they were struggling with communication on both ends; neither spoke the other's native tongue.

The flight attendant looked to the crowd of us waiting for our flights and asked if anyone could speak Vietnamese. I was the closest one to the flight attendant, but I felt myself freeze up. I could not bring myself to speak up. It was like I was frozen in place. I knew I definitely could have stepped in and facilitated the conversation, but with a bit of struggling to find the right words. This fear of failure and non-authenticity held me back. There was a sort of shyness or reluctance that suddenly overcame me and grounded me in my spot. I did not want to walk away, but I also did not want to jump in and help. I sort of felt like I was not completely right for the job. I could imagine myself trying to help them, but then undoubtedly tripping over words and pronouncing things wrong or weirdly, in my non-perfect accent. I guess I was shy, embarrassed, and vulnerable. I feared I would not do a good job.

However, this created a dilemma for me. I felt like a hypocrite. I have always wanted to better my Vietnamese language and make an effort to engage in Vietnamese culture, but there I was, just sitting idly by while another girl offered to help them. She was perfect. She spoke to them completely naturally. I was jealous. I am still uncomfortable with who I am; I am a person with shards of different cultures, neither here nor there. These are the moments that make me want to fit into a mold, to be one with a national community. It is something to which many people hold dear and can relate.

The problem that I mainly struggle with is uncertainty. The feeling of ambiguity, a lack of direction and control. True acceptance of who I am means being okay with that uncertainty. However, this is difficult because we are all hardwired to latch onto something—to find answers and belong. Sometimes I think I need to be okay with uncertainty and the indefinite, because identity and community are not straight lines. Identity is not black and white. Yet I am constantly in a state of uncertainty, navigating my way through this world in search of acceptance.

Chapter 5

Shame, Shame, Shame

Distinguishable Me

Indistinguishable, clumped together, forever mistaken
for someone else.
If *all Asians look the same*, then why
do I feel so like *me*?

My thoughts, feelings, states
of being are so intense, so real, so strong that
sometimes my emotions feel like they could
EXPLODE.

I feel colors inside me that
don't even exist, aren't even invented
yet. I feel colors inside me that
are loud, delicious, rough.

I am an individual, a
human, a *human*
—distinguishable.

invisible

have you ever had someone
look at you and
not even see you?

look right through you
like nothing is there—
too unimportant,
too inferior,
too much a waste of space.

i start to notice
that it's not just me
who's invisible. other
people who look like me
are sometimes invisible, too.

i have been in a crowded room
of White Americans,
and the only people they talk to
are people who look like them.
maybe i'm wrong.

look, i'm not making any accusations
but what more can i do when
no matter how much i try to talk,
they treat me with utter disregard?

i don't want to believe the
sad truth that it's related to my race
but when the other asian person

gets ignored too,
what am i supposed to think?

i can't help but feel
i'm pushed into the corner
forgotten,
invisible,
unwelcome.

i don't want to jump to conclusions
or make any accusations,
but over and over i have seen
my race pushed out,
looked over, made
invisible.

I Wish I Were White

I know I'm not the only one
who's wished to be another race.
Life just seems easier, luckier,
better on the other side.

I used to think life would be different,
I would be more beautiful,
more confident, more open
to taking chances.

I feel there's a certain image
I'm confined to, expected
to be shy, quiet, good
at math.

The stereotypes make me feel
limited in the ways that
I express myself.
They quiet my voice.

I've somehow fallen into
this exact trap,
found myself believing
my own inferiority—

somehow, put myself in
the very box I claim to hate.

The Power of a Name

Hats, Shoes, Nail Polish,
all these things can
help answer the question:
who are you in this world?

They're a part of your identity,
distinguishable details that
Define, Categorize, Describe.

A name, however, can also tell a story.
Where in the world are you from—
which continent or country,
which region or town?

I sometimes feel ashamed
of my birth-given name
It made me different,
hard for others to pronounce.

Vermin

I am a pest in this country.
Came from the outside,
born outside this nation's soil.

Some people consider me
vermin, filth, try to cast me out, but
let me contaminate the ground more.

Let me spread the sickness that is my culture
In the country that you deem so welcoming.
For I, too, am a part of this nation now.

Chapter 6

Microaggressions

BUT WHERE ARE YOU *REALLY* FROM?
"What is your culture? I mean where are you from? Like . . . originally from? You know, my husband's Chinese and I lived in China for a couple years."

A woman once asked me this question. I knew what she was trying to ask me, and I thought that it was completely valid to ask me where I was from. She must have been nervous when asking me this question because it seemed like she needed to prove herself to me toward the end of her rambling. The fact that she brought up her Chinese husband seemed like she wanted to show me that we had a connection somehow. Yet, her attempt at a connection created more space between us. I consider myself both Vietnamese and American, and I take pride in both nations. Because I am so passionate about Vietnam and crave a need for individuality, I suddenly felt very defensive about my culture. Because I am also passionate about America, I was also defensive that she thought I was not American. This led to me interpreting her effort at connection as an ignorant assumption that I was a Chinese foreigner. I felt like she was generalizing me by diminishing my Vietnamese roots and immediately thinking that I did not belong in America. I am patriotic, after all, but I knew her intent was not to be malicious. I reasoned that if she was trying to make an effort to learn and understand, I should not hold it against her.

I tried to hold back any resentment against her, but I remember being bothered by her question later that day. I am just too proud to be Vietnamese *and* American. In my unsettlement, I allowed the resentment to boil over and process my feelings. I thought, *Yes, asking about my origins and background is valid, but trying to relate by saying she knew someone of the same race was not. There were so many other ways to ask. Telling me that she had a Chinese friend or a Japanese husband didn't really accomplish much for me. I resonated with neither of those countries, and it was awkward for her to assume that just because I am Asian, I am inherently Chinese. Also, why did she assume I was a foreigner?*

I allowed my thoughts to trail and did not think of the situation for another few months. Reflecting back now, she may not have even made an assumption, but rather an attempt to signal her acceptance of and appreciation for ethnic diversity. Even with good intentions, the phrasing of the question came from a place of ignorance and unintentional microaggressions. I think it is important to know how to demonstrate that you are open-minded and willing to learn about different backgrounds—without making assumptions.

Ignorance is not intentionally malicious, but it illustrates the importance of cultural education. Personally, this question also brings up a lot of anxiety because my answer to "Where are you from?" is complicated. Simply telling someone that I am from Vietnam or from America would not fully do my true identity justice, but at the same time, who wants to hear my whole life story? Is giving them the longer version of my answer worth it? Would they even care? When I first came to America, I used to tell people I was from Vietnam. After the first three years of staying in America, I used to tell people I was from Houston. Up until recently, I always opted for the quicker option: "Yeah, I'm from Houston." It was easy and it made me feel like I fit in, like I belonged here. Now, I am proud to say that I am from both Vietnam and America. It feels more all-encompassing and truer to who I really am.

People's origins are usually very personally significant, which is why the word "patriotism" even exists. People generally love national representation and have great pride for their roots. Events like the FIFA World Cup and Miss Universe are so universally loved and supported because individuals bond over national pride while competing with other nations. This is also why it is important to not assume others' backgrounds, which applies to any aspect of a person, not just ethnicity or race. Keeping an open mind and empathizing with others allows for more human connection and cultural awareness.

CHINESE WHISPERS

During primary school, or elementary school, I studied at the British International School in Saigon, Vietnam. When I was in Year 2, my absolute favorite game to play was called "Chinese Whispers." This game is more commonly known in the United States as "Telephone," a game in which people sit in a circle, and one person starts off by whispering a sentence in the next person's ear. The aim of the game is to see how far the sentence makes it through the circle before it gets distorted by word of mouth. The fun of the game is seeing what sentences people end up with after the whisper chain. I thought it was the best game, because all the sentences ended up being so funny by the time we got to the last person in the circle. Whenever we had break time, I would wish, *Please be Chinese Whispers, please be Chinese Whispers,* over and over in my mind. Whenever a teacher gave us the option of which game to play, we would all choose Chinese Whispers.

Our white teachers taught us a game called Chinese Whispers, and no one batted an eye regarding the name. To be fair, my classmates and I were all very young. We did not know better, and we were not taught better. We were taught a fun game and then moved on with our lives and grew up. I had moved on with my life too, but I always looked back fondly on childhood games of Chinese Whispers. I was recently reminiscing with some childhood friends about our primary school, and our favorite game came up. That was the moment it clicked in our minds. I thought, *Wait, Chinese Whispers actually sounds kind of racist.* Realization slowly dawned on all our faces. It was a ridiculous moment—a revelation after all these years, over a decade of our lives. Suddenly, the memory of our beloved game and the memory of our old beloved teachers turned sour.

A few days later, I thought of our realization and could not get it out of my mind. I immediately did some research on the game Chinese Whispers. Apparently, the word "Chinese" was supposed to indicate Western confusion and incomprehension centuries ago. Historians traced this word back all the way to the seventeenth century, when Europeans and Chinese people made contact for one of the first times and Europeans were unable to understand China's culture and worldview. To historians, the use of the phrase "Chinese whispers" suggested the idea that the language of Chinese itself was not understandable (Ballaster). So, the name made sense for the game, intended to show how a phrase or a sentence becomes garbled and incomprehensible when passed on through the circle.

I think it was originally an acceptable name for the game, but in our world today, it is outdated. Evidently, there are others who think so too, because I have not heard anyone call it Chinese Whispers for a while. Then again, I also have been living in America, in which the name is always Telephone. Old traditions and ideals are just that—old. They can be worthy of respect, but there must also be an opportunity to learn and grow from them. Denoting incomprehensibility as Chinese can be seen as insensitive. After all, Chinese is understandable to millions of people in the world. Simply subjecting a pervasive language to a stereotype, and a negative one at that, serves to devalue a language and its culture. This revelation has taught me that appreciating different cultures and keeping an open mind is helpful in avoiding cultural insensitivity and stereotypes. Even though I am not Chinese, this matters to me because of how strongly I feel toward my own cultural and identity—I would not want anyone to devalue or stereotype it.

WORKS CITED

Ballaster, Rosalind (2005). *Fabulous Orients: fictions of the East in England, 1662–1785*. Oxford University Press. pp. 202–3. ISBN 0-19-926733-2

Identity Fraud

Once, mistaken for someone else.
Thought me to be a vicious tormentor,
they cried and they hated me
for offenses I did not commit.

You've got the wrong person,
I wanted to scream
but it was too little, too late.
I had already been taken prisoner, berated

for something I did not do.
Thought to be someone else
who looked like me.
Apologies were communicated,

all forgiven. But one thing
keeps me up at night—
how does someone forget
the face of their bully?

Part 2

What In the World Is Happening to Us?

Chapter 7

In the Media

ASIANS ARE NOT SAFE

One song that has always really resonated with me and made me feel better is *Safe* by Korean rapper Dumbfoundead, whose real name is Jonathan Park. When I first heard this song, I had just been in America for a year or two, and it shocked me because it drew attention to issues that I thought only I had noticed. The song explores Asian under-representation and misrepresentation in the media. In the music video, Dumbfoundead edits his face onto actors in several different iconic scenes from movies and television shows such as *Titanic, The Pirates of the Caribbean,* and *Friends.* For example, in one scene of the montage, his face takes Leonardo DiCaprio's face while Jack holds Rose on the boat in *Titanic.*

The music video depicted a jarring exposure to the lack of Asian representation in my favorite Hollywood movies. The montage of Park's face juxtaposed with the actors I know and love truly calls attention to Hollywood whitewashing. Other than the music video, I also loved the song's lyrics. The lines in *Safe* send the message that society and entertainment see Asians as "safe," and that we are so much more than that. The song's chorus repeats, "You took me as safe / That was your first mistake / Who said I was safe" (Park). Other lyrics from the song emphasize the disparity in racial representation in Western entertainment: "The other night I watched the Oscars and the roster of the only yellow men were all statues / We a quarter of the population" (Park). In this particular line, Park comments on how no Asian-Americans have won an Oscar in recent years.

I took the message of the song to heart. In high school, I was a theater kid who wrote and performed in plays and loved to sing and make art. To me, the song's message hit close to home. As an avid fan of the arts and entertainment, I was finally not the only one who had noticed how misrepresented or underrepresented I had been in the media. I saw the nuanced crevices of the world rather than the sheltered bubble that I'd lived in, but I thought I was the only one. Since discovering Dumbfoundead, I found a whole community of people trying to create a movement for Asian-American exposure. This realization from Park's song gave me a new lens through which to view the world. Instead of standing idly by and taking discrimination as is, I have learned how to voice my opinions and try to create social change for our community.

Long Duk Dong

A sidekick, a background character,
forced to repeatedly embody
tired and offensive stereotypes.

Hollywood has built a successful empire
on Asian tropes like
the goofy Chinese immigrant,
Long Duk Dong from *Sixteen Candles*.

Long Duk Dong
is beloved, popular, and funny.
Exploiting these stereotypes,
monopolizing and gaining
at the expense of
another's culture.

Asian tropes paraded
around for decades
Yet no one
batted an eye until now.

I guess it's okay when
it brings in money at the box office.

That Asian Movie

When a movie has more than
two minority leads,
it's immediately an
Asian movie or *black movie.*

The same doesn't apply to
movies with white leads—
they're just considered normal,
just what you're used to seeing.

And what's worse is the film tropes
that Asian-Americans play out—
the math nerd, the submissive
Asian woman.

Crazy Rich Asians was a milestone
But when will I watch a movie
with a big Asian cast that's
just considered normal?

Chapter 8

Asian-American Underrepresentation in Hollywood

In the United States, Asian-Americans make up 5.6 percent of the population, but in Hollywood, Asians represent less than 3 percent of the industry (Lam). Throughout film history, Asians actors have been "forced to repeatedly embody tired and offensive stereotypes, and they are frequently relegated to the role of a sidekick or background character" (Lopez 6). Hollywood has long found success in playing out Asian tropes such as the goofy Chinese immigrant Long Duk Dong from *Sixteen Candles,* released in 1984. The character was initially met with huge success as audiences found comedy in his goofy "foreign" antics. Since then, Hollywood has continued to build on the trope and found great box office success in exploiting these stereotypes for comedy and media attention (Davé 142). Asian tropes have been paraded for decades, and no one has batted an eye; stereotypical Asian roles have become normalized. Not only is there a disparity between Asian and white actors, but also between Asian and white filmmakers. The Hollywood film industry as a whole largely underrepresents the Asian-American community.

Out of seven hundred top-grossing films in 2014, only nineteen directors were Asian (2.4 percent) (Smith). Over the past ten years, there was virtually no change in the number of Asian directors in Hollywood, according to a report released in 2017 by the Media, Diversity, and Social Change Initiative at the University of Southern California (USC) Annenberg School for Communication and Journalism. The report found that as of 2017, only 3.4 percent of American filmmakers were Asian (Smith). Although Asians have recently received more jobs in Hollywood, "Asian actors and filmmakers are not invading Hollywood as much as they are finally being admitted into Hollywood—under very specific conditions and for very specific roles" (Pham 122).

Mainstream Hollywood has lumped all Asians together, neglecting the different, distinct countries in Asia. Mainstream Asian roles follow the same trope (Pham 123). Inaccurate and stereotypical perceptions of Asians in Hollywood, however, have implications for conformity, participation, and representation. The normalization of Asian stereotypes influences the way Asian-Americans are perceived by others and themselves, which leads to underrepresentation of Asians in Hollywood.

The eighty-seventh Academy Awards in 2015 sparked a lot of backlash. Social media activist April Reign started the hashtag #OscarsSoWhite after realizing no actors of color were nominated. The hashtag quickly caught on and there was a lot of discussion about Hollywood's whitewashing, or "the tendency of media to be dominated by white characters, played by white actors, navigating their way through a story that will likely resonate most deeply with white audiences, based on their experiences and worldviews" (Andrist).

Whitewashing refers to both the misrepresentation of characters of color and the domination of white characters and actors in films. Whitewashing also occurs when white actors are cast by directors to play originally non-white roles and characters. For example, the casting of Scarlett Johansson in *Ghost in the Shell* received a lot of outrage and media attention. *Ghost in the Shell* is based on a Japanese manga in which the characters are Asian, and many critics found that it would have been more fitting for an Asian actor to have played the role. However, in Hollywood, Asians are only seen in the same few specific roles.

The specific roles Asian-Americans are forced to play out are tropes. Some common tropes are that Asians are seen as "foreign," non-threatening, and as comic relief (Mehta). Because this is the case, bigger or more nuanced roles are left for white people, as they do not face the same preconceived notions. In Hollywood, Asian (including Indian) men specifically are seen as emasculated and comical. On *The Big Bang Theory*, Raj plays out the Asian/Indian trope of being highly intelligent, yet being unable to interact with females in a romantic way. Raj is a brilliant astrophysicist, yet he is highly socially awkward when interacting with women unless he is intoxicated. When people are intoxicated, they lose their inhibitions, showing more of their true personality. The show portrays Asian men as if they are only themselves with the help of alcohol, and are otherwise socially incapable and less desirable.

The case is the same for Asian actresses who play out certain stereotypes: the exotic sexy woman who cannot speak English, the fragile foreigner, the quiet nerd, and so on (Smith). These roles are most prevalent for Asian actors; seldom do they play any other major roles. This has been the case in Hollywood for decades, with little to no change in past years, which only reinforces the tropes. Actresses Anna May Wong and Lucy Liu are both known to play Asian "dragon ladies" who are domineering but physically attractive. Anna May Wong was typecast as a dragon lady and played these roles in the 1920s; she temporarily left the United States and Hollywood to act in Europe and escape the typecast. Actress Lucy Liu has also been accused of constantly playing this polarizing stereotype. Asian women are also typecast as prostitutes and sex workers. One of the most famous film examples of an Asian woman sexually offering herself to white men is the Vietnamese sex worker with the line "me love you long time" in the 1987 film *Full Metal Jacket* (Nittle).

These stereotypical Asian roles in Hollywood have become so normalized that Asians themselves limit their own opportunities by the way they perceive themselves. Critics strongly objected to the whitewashed casting choices in *Ghost in the Shell*. Whereas objection was the general consensus, there were also opinions supporting the whitewashing. For example, the original manga producer Sam Yoshiba said, "Looking at her career so far, I think Scarlett Johansson is well cast. She has the cyberpunk feel. And we never imagined it would be a Japanese actress in the first place." He added, "This is a chance for a Japanese property to be seen around the world" (Kilday). Yoshiba, an Asian man, diminished the value of Asians so much that Asian actors were not even an option for casting. In this way, he puts white people on a pedestal.

This illustrates the concept of the Asian inferiority complex toward white people. In Asia, white people are seen as superior in many aspects: politics, media, sports, and beauty (Haider). In Asian sports, a white coach is more desirable than an Asian one because they are perceived as having more knowledge. As for beauty, Western features are considered more beautiful as Asians now get plastic surgery for the Western double eyelid (Haider). Skin bleaching is also prevalent in Asia.

Where there are Asian critics who support Hollywood whitewashing, there are also those who understand the concept of Asian inferiority. Guy Aoki, Founding President of Media Action Network for Asian Americans (MANAA), comments, "Many in Japan have been so brainwashed by Western culture that they've developed an inferiority complex about their own. They assume that in order for an American film to be successful, it has to star a white actor" (Kilday). Because Asians are so used to seeing white actors in every role, it has been normalized and no one questions it or takes action. This normalization has led to the idea that Asian underrepresentation in Hollywood is partly due to the mentality of the Asian actors themselves; they see themselves in the set roles they have grown up watching and conforming to what society has set out for them.

Other factors that lead to misconstrued perceptions of Asians is that they have the reputation as the "model minority." The model minority stereotype is that Asians are seen as submissive, will never question authority, and will always do as they are told (Tribune News Service). The perception that Asians are the "model minority" leads some filmmakers to have trouble picturing Asians in a more dominant role. When multiple filmmakers were asked why they did not cast an Asian in an Asian role, they simply replied that "part of the problem is that Asians don't fit the studio chiefs' vision of a leading man," since there is a perception that Asians will dutifully carry out subordinate tasks without question (Tribune News Service). Korean American actor Edward Hong expresses, "We are always the model minority" (Tribune News Service).

Many voices have expressed their dissent for the unequal treatment of Asian-American actors in Hollywood. The issue has upset many people, including Nancy Wang Yuen, a professor at Biola University: "There is a bias against Asian Americans, I feel like we are invisible in society. We are nondescript and, in a way, dehumanized by not existing in scenes or having speaking roles. We are just part of the backdrop" (Tribune News Service). The disparity of Asian opportunities on the big screen still leaves the community unsettled, yet Hollywood makes no moves for change.

Because Hollywood has barely progressed toward greater Asian representation, whitewashing continues to influence the way Asian-Americans are represented to the masses, thus normalizing tropes. However, a show featuring an Asian main cast was recently released. *Fresh Off the Boat* is an American sitcom series featuring an all-Asian main cast that centers around an Asian-American family in Orlando, Florida. The series is a milestone for the Asian-American community—for the first time, Asians are getting the spotlight in a television series. Though this shows a positive improvement for the Asian-white actor gap, the series reinforces many Asian stereotypes, which further feeds into the set roles of Asians in Hollywood films. After the release of its first season, the series received some criticism of its title. In the United States, "fresh off the boat" (FOB) refers to immigrants in the United States who continue their cultural ideologies and practices without assimilating into American culture, language, and practices. Twitter user @KaitlynYin claims "Fresh Off the Boat normalizes the term. Whites think it's acceptable to use without realizing historical origins" (Lopez 2).

Although the show's lively storyline and characters strive to redeem the phrase "fresh off the boat," the show itself still fails to bridge the Hollywood diversity disparity. The stereotypes are mainly exhibited through the role of the mother in the family, in which the actress puts on a fake stereotypical Chinese accent and acts out Asian stereotypes. For example, the mom yells at clerks at the grocery store, is a "tiger mom" to the kids, and is frugal with money. This is the first time Asians got a shot at the big screen, but the show is not a very encompassing representation of the Asian-American community. Even though Asians have started to break through with *Fresh Off the Boat*, the show is facing potential cancellation, taking away the one show which gave Asians some media attention, regardless of its misrepresentations. The show serves as one of the only forms of mainstream Asian-American representation on television.

For the general public that does not understand the nuance of Asian underrepresentation, the stereotypes in the show reinforce their preconceived beliefs. This makes the show's renewal vital and the implication very meaningful—the show speaks for 5.6 percent of the United States' population as no other television shows give Asian-Americans exactly the same type of voice (Mazzucato). A show about an Asian-American family is not treated like a show about a white family—they have to fight much harder to get and "keep a seat at the table" (Mazzucato).

While conformity of roles is the issue, many negative implications and consequences arise from nonconformity. American television series *Master of None* released an episode called "Indians on TV" in 2015 that illustrates how directors casting for typically Asian roles look for actors to play into the tropes. The episode shows character Dev who is an actor auditioning for the role of "unnamed cab driver." At the end of his audition, the directors refuse to cast him because his American accent was "not exactly what they were looking for" (Mehta). Minutes later, another Indian actor (Ravi) walks out and tells Dev that he got the role because he put on an Indian accent. Ravi does not actually have a real Indian accent; he simply put it on to get the role in the audition. The episode raises an important issue here, as Dev is faced with a cultural and professional dilemma: performing with the accent would guarantee him a chance to breakthrough into the Hollywood industry, but it denies him of his individuality, experiences, and sense of self (Davé 142). As more research is done about the reasons for the racial hierarchies in mass media, the issue can be examined through the lens of race and language (Davé 144). The episode explores many issues of diversity and inclusion in Hollywood through a discussion of issues of racism and representation.

This one episode is a prime meta example of the inequality Asian-Americans face in Hollywood. Mehta, exasperated, expresses "there's only space for one brown person per show; otherwise white people will feel alienated, even though that's how I feel watching TV *literally all the time*" (Mehta). The episode also raises the concept of how "there can't be two." Dev faces the problem of directors refusing to cast more than one Indian in a show because then it will be known as an "Indian people show," even though shows that have only white actors are not seen as a "white people show" (Mehta). Asian and Indian roles are played through tropes, so they serve as comic relief and fill very specific roles for which films or shows usually have a single spot. Because these are the only available roles for Asians, they pigeonhole themselves for success.

Asian actors hold their own identities back for success, as they are hesitant to speak out or raise conflict and not receive a role at all. One line from Dev's agent in the "Indians on TV" expresses how Asians need to survive in the American film industry: "I'm trying to get this *Friends* money, Dev, and you fuckin' it up." Here, she is commenting on the fact that by objecting and refusing to conform to tropes of American directors, Dev is passing up on many opportunities to earn money. She also goes on to add that if she had complained about every little racist situation she had faced in her career, she would not be where she was now. Maitri Mehta, an Indian-American, shares the sentiment:

In my own life, I have to pick my battles and weigh each risk carefully: by speaking up, I feel like I am doing the right thing, but it also could jeopardize my opportunities with people in power. This could be as small as speaking up against microaggressions from bosses, college professors, even dudes I meet at bars. But it's not the responsibility of the oppressed to change the behaviors of the oppressor; that theme is potent in "Indians on TV," with Dev's desire to incite change conflicting with the reality of life (Mehta).

The opinions of various Asians regarding racial microaggressions expose a big problem. In order to survive, Asians are forced to compromise their own values and personalities to conform to a society that does not accept their true selves.

Although Asian underrepresentation and misrepresentation in Hollywood are still dire, there has been a bit of traction in the Asian film industry. Some actors who do not view the issue as pressing have downplayed the diversity controversy, such as Michael Caine and Julie Delpy. In an interview with a French journalist, Academy Award nominee Charlotte Rampling received backlash for saying that "perhaps the black actors did not deserve" nominations (Ryan). The public criticism in these cases is evidence of that traction.

A movement for boycott arose in response to the Academy Awards nominating all white actors in lead and supporting categories for the second consecutive year. Actor Spike Lee announced on his Instagram that he and his wife "[could] not support" the Academy Awards' whitewashing and would not attend the ceremony (Ryan). Actors Will Smith and Jada Pinkett-Smith announced their intention to boycott during a Good Morning America interview and a video on Facebook (Ryan). Other A-list Hollywood actors have supported the dissent, such as George Clooney, Reese Witherspoon, Don Cheadle, and Lupita Nyong'o. Even President Obama expressed concern for Hollywood's diversity issue (Ryan). These strong influences inspired and paved the way for other influential people to create stronger and more solid solutions.

Beyond boycotts and public objection, the #OscarsSoWhite and #MeToo movements led to the creation of a contract clause called the Inclusion Rider. The concept originated from Stacy Smith, the founder and director of USC's Annenberg Inclusion Initiative. She worked with attorneys from the law firm Cohen Milstein on how to integrate diversity and inclusion into Hollywood laws (Judkis). The idea has quickly gained attention since its announcement in a 2016 TED talk. The Inclusion Rider is described as follows:

A way to make Hollywood more equitable. Actors sign contracts when they are cast in films, and they have the ability to negotiate for riders, or additional provisions. An inclusion rider is a stipulation that the cast and/or the crew in a film reflect real demographics, including a proportionate number of women, minorities, LGBTQ individuals, and people with disabilities (Judkis).

Essentially, the Inclusion Rider encourages actors to lay out requirements in their contracts that promote diversity and inclusion. Highly influential actors can use their name to drastically leverage better representation in film. This legal initiative creates firm rules and would lead to more progress, diversity, and inclusion to address the Asian Hollywood disparity.

The movement for directors to stop relying on tropes and give Asians more representative roles has begun. Director Taika Waititi is set to direct a film adaptation of the manga *Akira*. Unlike past manga adaptations that have been whitewashed such as *Death Note*, Waititi understands the diversity issue and intends to defy Asian tropes (Trumbore). "Actually [casting] Asian teenagers would be the way to do it for me and probably [young people with] unfound, untapped talent. Yeah, I'd probably want to take it a bit back more toward the books" (Trumbore). Waititi wants to keep the adaptation as authentic and close to the books as possible, seemingly in response to the whitewashing problem in Hollywood.

Crazy Rich Asians, directed by Jon M. Chu, is another film featuring an all-Asian cast. The main female lead, Constance Wu, was actually set to be played by a white actress, but Chu decided to cast Wu instead (Jagota). Asian-American Vrinda Jagota comments that "*Crazy Rich Asians* is obviously still very showy and class-exclusive, but as an Asian American who has literally never seen a movie like this on the big screen in my lifetime, I'll take what I can get" (Jagota). This statement shows the severity of Asian-American underrepresentation in Hollywood. Although there has been a small movement to close the gap between the number of white actors to Asian actors in Hollywood, more action needs to be taken. Fortunately, some older television shows like *Heroes* and *Lost* have featured various main Asian leads, which is a win for Hollywood diversity casting. *Lost*'s Korean couple Soo Kwon and Sun were striking in portraying Asian characters as fully-fledged human beings with a wide array of emotions and experiences. The couple's complex storyline was a riveting part of the highly acclaimed TV show.

Ultimately, a large disparity between the number of Asian-Americans and white people in Hollywood still exists. Therefore, a large community of the United States is still inadequately represented in one of the largest mass media industries. Feelings of neglect and injustice have arisen among the Asian-American community, which represents a decent portion of the American population. Other implications include conformity issues, stereotypes, and negative self-perception. The lack of inclusion of Asians in Hollywood is due to many factors. Asians' perception of themselves and others' perception of them lead to conformity, stereotypical Asian roles, and the normalization of tropes, thus limiting opportunities overall. The Asian inferiority complex, the "model minority" stereotype, and conformity of roles and its implications are major factors leading to Asian underrepresentation in Hollywood. Despite recent, positive movements toward diverse representation in Hollywood, the rate of change has been slow and small.

WORKS CITED

Andrist, Lester. "What Is Whitewashing and Why Does It Matter?" @TheSocyCinema, 22 Feb. 2015, www.thesociologicalcinema.com/blog/what-is-whitewashing.

Davé, Shilpa. "Racial Accents, Hollywood Casting, and Asian American Studies." Cinema Journal 56.3 (2017): 142,147,153. ProQuest. Web. 23 Apr. 2018.

Haider, Umair. "What's with the South Asian Inferiority Complex?" Blogs, 5 May 2012, blogs.tribune.com.pk/story/11456/whats-with-the-south-asian-inferiority-complex/.

Jagota, Vrinda. "'Crazy Rich Asians' Is The First Hollywood Movie With An All-Asian Cast In 25 Years." PAPER, PAPER, 24 Apr. 2018, www.papermag.com/crazy-rich-asians-trailer-2562672449.html.

Judkis, Maura, and Stephanie Merry. "What Is an Inclusion Rider? Michael B. Jordan Is Taking on Frances McDormand's Oscars Proposal." The Washington Post, WP Company, 8 Mar. 2018, www.washingtonpost.com/news/arts-and-entertainment/wp/2018/03/05/what-is-an-inclusion-rider-explaining-frances-mcdormands-call-to-action-at-the-oscars/?noredirect=on&utm_term=.de65d9196302.

Kilday, Gregg. "'Ghost in the Shell': How a Complex Concept, 'Whitewashing' and Critics Kept Crowds Away." The Hollywood Reporter, The Hollywood Reporter, 2 Apr. 2017, www.hollywoodreporter.com/heat-vision/ghost-shell-how-a-complex-concept-whitewashing-critics-kept-crowds-away-990661.

Lam, Charles. "Number of Asian Hollywood Directors Saw Virtually 'No Change' in 10 Years: Report." NBCNews.com, NBCUniversal News Group, 1 Feb. 2017, www.nbcnews.com/news/asian-america/number-asian-hollywood-directors-no-change-10-years-report-n715551.

Lopez, Lori Kido. "Introduction: The Role of Asian American Media Activism." *Asian American Media Activism: Fighting* for Cultural Citizenship, NYU Press, New York, 2016, pp. 1–34. JSTOR, www.jstor.org/stable/j.ctt1803zph.4.

Mazzucato, Olivia. "Second Take: 'Fresh Off the Boat's' Representational Significance Merits Its Renewal." Daily Bruin, 16 Apr. 2018, dailybruin.com/2018/04/16/second-take-fresh-off-the-boats-representational-significance-merits-its-renewal/.

Mehta, Maitri. "'Master Of None' Addresses Discrimination Head On." Bustle, Bustle, 19 Apr. 2018, www.bustle.com/articles/122532-aziz-ansaris-master-of-none-episode-indians-on-tv-gets-representation-painfully-right.

Pham, Minh-Ha T. "The Asian Invasion (of Multiculturalism) in Hollywood." Journal of Popular Film & Television 32.3 (2004): 121-31. ProQuest. Web. 23 Apr. 2018.

Ryan, Patrick. "#OscarsSoWhite Controversy: What You Need to Know." USA Today, Gannett Satellite Information Network, 2 Feb. 2016, www.usatoday.com/story/life/movies/2016/02/02/oscars-academy-award-nominations-diversity/79645542/.

Smith, Stacy L, and Marc Choueti. Inequality in 700 Popular Films: Examining Portrayals of Gender, Race, & LGBT Status from 2007 to 2014. University of Southern California, 2015, pp. 1–30, Inequality in 700 Popular Films: Examining Portrayals of Gender, Race, & LGBT Status from 2007 to 2014.

Tribune News Service. "For Asian Actors, Few Leading Roles and Lower Pay." Honolulu Star-Advertiser, 12 July 2017, www.star-advertiser.com/2017/07/12/breaking-news/for-asian-actors-few-leading-roles-and-lower-pay/.

Trumbore, Dave. "Taika Waititi Shares Casting Plans for Possible 'Akira' Adaptation." Collider, Collider, 11 Oct. 2017, collider.com/taika-waititi-akira-movie-cast/.

Nittle, Nadra Kareem. "Why Hollywood Should Drop These 5 Asian American Stereotypes." *ThoughtCo*, ThoughtCo, 24 June 2019, www.thoughtco.com/asian-american-stereotypes-in-t-film-2834652.

Chapter 9

Get Me Out of This Box

CAN ASIANS BE SEXY?
"Do you like Asian men? No, thank you. You like Asian men? I don't even like Chinese food [. . .] I don't eat what I can't pronounce."

This is a controversial bit in one of Steve Harvey's comedy shows that went viral in January of 2017. In Harvey's skit, he finds himself extremely funny, laughing uncontrollably at his attempt at a joke. His racist joke at the expense of Asian men faced much criticism and outrage from the Asian American community, including New York politicians and *Fresh Off The Boat* author Eddie Huang. He then issued a typical PR apology: "I offer my humblest apology for offending anyone, particularly those in the Asian community. It was not my intention, and the humor was not meant with any malice or disrespect whatsoever" (Twitter @iamsteveharvey). I say that this is a typical PR apology, because initially, Harvey responded, "You know they're kinda beating me up on the internet right now for no reason, but ya know that's life ain't it." He clearly showed no remorse about his joke or his blatant racism against Asian men.

There are many Asians who do not get personally offended by racist jokes like this. They claim that they "have been hearing it [their] whole life." This nonchalance goes to show that jokes at the expense of Asian-Americans have become so normalized that, in some cases, it no longer affects the victim. Severe double standards exist with regard to racist jokes. It seems that jokes about the Asian-American community are a norm, but imagine if the roles were switched and an Asian Steve Harvey said these things about black people on national television:

"Excuse me, do you like black men? No, thank you."

It would be safe to assume, looking at America's progressiveness in recent years, that that Asian man's career would be over. He would receive death threats and would probably not be able to book another job, and there would be significantly more outrage. This would be a significant positive for marginalized groups, reflecting increasing inclusivity and appreciation for diversity. However, since the original joke was about Asians, it is not as big of a deal, showing that there is still much work to be done. Because, you know, it is just a joke, and Asians are like the punching bags of society. Eddie Huang, author of *Fresh Off The Boat* and inspiration for the main protagonist of the TV adaption, effectively summarizes Harvey's racist joke. "[Steve Harvey] speaks openly about issues facing the black community, he is a man of God, and he has a huge platform to speak from. Yet, he perpetuates the emasculation of Asian men regardless of how hypocritical it is" (Eddie Huang, *New York Times*). Harvey emasculated Asian men and showed no remorse for it. His intentions were not seemingly malicious, but it goes to show the need for more education and awareness.

The subtle racism and microaggressions targeting the sexuality and attractiveness of Asian men extend not only to comedy skits, but also to major movements like #OscarsSoWhite. This event was supposed to be an event of diversity and inclusion, but at the second annual Oscars So White, Sacha Baron Cohen makes a racist joke about Asian men: "All people of all colors . . . how come there is no Oscar for them very hardworking little yellow people with tiny dongs, you know, them minions." Here, Cohen makes a *Despicable Me* reference and a reference to the age-old joke about Asian men's genitals. The juxtaposition of the ignorance of Cohen's joke and an event meant to encourage diversity and inclusion in Hollywood shows an urgent need for further education. Unfortunately, in the moment, Cohen's racist jokes garnered laughs from the audience and seemed to be entirely unoffensive.

However, a myriad of outraged responses broke out on Twitter shortly after. Examples included actor Jeffrey Wright's tweet on Twitter, complaining about Cohen's "Half-assed Asian joke, #oscars, and then preach about diversity? #loseme." *Glee* and *Shadowhunters* actor Harry Shum Jr.'s tweeted, "Lazy, uncreative joke after a brilliant monologue @chrisrock #diversitymyass." Lastly, Constance Wu shared a text from a friend that read, "the joke shows that there are just no actual consequences to making fun [of] and degrading Asians. So that in an entire broadcast totally obsessed with racism and diversity, throwing Asians under the bus is totally fine." Many high-profile figures have noticed Hollywood's insensitivity toward Asian-Americans.

Research has been conducted on the history of Asian stereotypes. The stereotype of Asians being good at math and are hardworking actually originated during the mid 1800s. During a section of MTV's web series Decoded, the history of male Asian emasculation is traced back:

To counteract the massive wave of important cheap Chinese labor, Asian men were subject to a series of target laws that systematically stripped them of rights that signified manhood, such as property ownership, job opportunities, and the ability to marry freely. The legislation worked hand-in-hand with the campaign on the cultural front, warning men and women of the yellow peril and peppering newspapers with caricatures that clearly showed these Chinese workers as less than regular men (MTV Webseries Decoded).

Stereotypes come from somewhere, and are often from age-old views; however, we are now in a new century and must move on from outdated and offensive cultural views. Significant statistical and anecdotal evidence demonstrates that Asian men take a hit in the dating pool because of perception bias. We rely on popular culture to shape popular opinion. Like the cartoonists of the nineteenth century, today's artists and entertainers have the power to articulate stereotypes about Asian men. Stereotypes such as *The Hangover*'s Mr. Chow, whose penis was mistaken for a shiitake mushroom, have been played out, and it is time to put a stop to them.

WORKS CITED

Higa, Ryan, director. *Can Asians Be Sexy? YouTube*, YouTube, 28 Jan. 2017, www.youtube.com/watch?v=dCP0Ohgl1RQ.

MTV Webseries Decoded

THE ASIAN N-WORD

In the era of "Linsanity," when ESPN wrote about Jeremy Lin and titled the article "A Chink in the Armor," some people still defended it as a joke. However, it is clear that the use of a racist joke in a non-comedic sports related article is entirely inappropriate. Not only is the placement of this joke inappropriate, but the title also uses one of the most racist slurs against Asians. The word "chink" is one of the most offensive slurs for Asians, but people either do not know or do not care. The word does not hold the same gravity. What if the word chink was switched out for the "n" word or another racist slur that people find more offensive? Society and mainstream media teach us that making racist jokes is not okay, except for racist Asian jokes.

The article immediately sparked outrage, and ESPN's apologetic response was speedy: "Last night, ESPN.com's mobile website posted an offensive headline referencing Jeremy Lin at 2:30 a.m. ET. The headline was removed at 3:05 a.m. ET. We are conducting a complete review of our cross-platform editorial procedures and are determining appropriate disciplinary action to ensure this does not happen again. We regret and apologize for this mistake." The language used here reflects a sense of avoidance. For example, ESPN.com's "mobile website" did the posting, not a writer or an editor.

ESPN provided no admission of wrongdoing or acknowledgment of the emotions hurt and the repercussions for the communities involved. The statement seems like one of defense—a typical PR apology rather than a real one. A real apology is issued when the perpetrator feels remorse and uses an empathetic tone; here, ESPN's tone is robotic, technical, logical, and direct: "this is what happened and we will try to fix it."

ESPN's problematic staff did not stop there. After posting the article, an ESPN news anchor used the same offensive term. After firing the writer of the article and suspending the news anchor, they issued another statement. "We again apologize especially to Mr. Lin. His accomplishments are a source of great pride to the Asian-American community, including the Asian-American employees at ESPN. Through self-examination, improved editorial practices and controls, and response to contrastive criticism, we will be better in the future" (CNN). This apology is heartfelt and much appreciated, but it is just too little, too late. The damage had already been done, and ESPN had offended a large group of people. The response to the lasting resentment toward the racist article title was also still problematic. The phrase "especially to the Asian-American employees at ESPN" is similar to another familiar apology many Asians have heard before: "Oh my gosh, I'm sorry for offending you! I love and appreciate your culture! I have a friend who is Asian and my nail lady is Asian!" Five years later, the article writer Anthony Federico is a priest. He said, "Looking back, I think God allowed this to happen to me to put me on a path to being a priest, a path that I was avoiding, I've never been happier"

(Washington Post). Federico made an honest mistake, and that is completely understandable.

But, enough with honest mistakes. It is now 2020, and the world can no longer be as ignorant. It is important now, more than ever, to think outside of one's own world, skin color, or culture. Now that it is 2020, the use of the Asian equivalent of the "n word" is no longer an honest mistake, but rather ignorance, a lack of education, and a lack of social consciousness. Mistakes and ignorance come from unconscious biases, toxic stereotypes, and microaggressions perpetuated over centuries. Even honest mistakes are reflective of ignorance. Negligence. Pleading guilty and pleading negligent are both equally bad. It is time to educate ourselves.

WORKS CITED

Zauzmer, Julie. "Fired by ESPN for a Racist Headline, He's Finding His Second Chance as a Catholic Priest." *The Washington Post*, WP Company, 2 Oct. 2017, www.washingtonpost.com/news/acts-of-faith/wp/2017/10/02/fired-by-espn-for-a-racist-headline-hes-finding-his-second-chance-as-a-catholic-priest/?arc404=true.

Chapter 10

Mistreatment

Liberty and Justice for All!

I still remember the day
the country I call my home
shattered my heart.
It'll take a while to forgive.

The day that a Vietnamese man
was violently dragged from a United airplane,
I was enraged and scared and appalled
to live in a country where
someone would think that kind of violence

acceptable.
The thing that still makes my stomach sick
isn't the actual mistreatment itself.
My heart still hasn't healed
because of the people of the United States

whose reactions were even more painful.
In response to screams and blood
and dragging a human like an animal,
they still dared to justify their actions.
How dare you.

How dare you justify
This physical violence,
violently forcing a man from a flight,
from a seat he had paid for.
The spin is sickening.

I really don't know how

to be comfortable
in my own skin
in the country I call home,
in the country that broke my heart.

I am left uncomfortable, unsafe,
unwelcome.

And America
still has the audacity to say
with liberty and justice for all.

Part 3

Acceptance and Resolution

Chapter 11

Citizenship Oath Swearing Ceremony

On June 1, 2019, I officially became an American citizen. In order to officially become an American citizen, I had to attend an oath swearing ceremony at the United States Citizenship and Immigration Services (USCIS) office. My ceremony was set to take place at 8:00 a.m. on June 1 and I was excited to finally become officially naturalized. In my mind, the ceremony did not seem like it was going to be a big event. This was because when I had first received the letter to attend the ceremony, it was written very formally and the government stamp on it made it seem steely and unemotional. Because of these notions that I had about the ceremony, I expected it to last maybe fifteen minutes, and that I would just be in and out. I did not expect it to be a big deal, so I went alone. That morning, my loud alarm buzzed at 7:15 a.m., right on schedule, and I lazily dragged myself out of my warm and comfortable bed. I proceeded with my usual routine—I brushed my teeth, scarfed down an apple, turned on my car, and drove fifteen minutes to get there. I sang along to the bops I was listening to on Spotify. Moving to America is one of the greatest things that has happened to me. This place makes up so much of who I am today. It has nurtured my unique self and voice, and I would not have it any other way. I am definitely proud to be an American, but I did not understand the gravity of the oath swearing ceremony until I actually got there.

When I pulled into the office driveway, I was immediately taken aback. It felt like I was entering a crowded festival or celebration. There were hundreds of people, forming a maze of numerous single-file lines snaking all around the office courtyard. When I got out of my car, my shock was only exacerbated. I had obviously missed the memo—I was the black sheep of the majestic party. There were whole families there and many friends, chattering excitedly in different languages and native tongues. Everyone waited excitedly and anxiously outside the office door. The energy in the USCIS courtyard that morning was palpable—the anticipation, nerves, jitters, elation, relief, and eagerness. It surrounded me, and I felt completely out of place. This oath swearing ceremony was a big deal to a lot of people.

It was strange being there. I felt somewhat out of place but at the same time, I related to the others around me. I was surrounded by a myriad of emotions, as if I could feel everyone's hearts beating around me.

Beat. Excitement. *Beat.* Nervousness. *Beat.* Warmth.

Goosebumps crept onto my arms and legs and emotion overwhelmed me. I was engulfed by the warmth and feelings of everyone around me. I refocused and took my place in line, weaving my way through the animated exhilaration and anxiety. At 8:00 a.m. sharp, a security guard called us in by group. We checked in and poured into the waiting room, the employees called our names and gave us our documents, and we waited for the ceremony to begin.

Sitting in the waiting room, I surveyed the crowd. There were people of all sorts of backgrounds and situations. Some anxiously shook their knees or tapped their armrests, and some were seemingly nonchalant and bored, like the teens in their Nike shorts with headphones in their ears and eyes glued to their phones. Some families were having hushed conversations while others were engaged in boisterous discussions. Others were resting their eyes, trying to nap before the ceremony—it was early, after all. Every sort of emotion seemed to be present in that room, and I was aware of all of it. Many of the people around me had fought tooth and nail to become a part of the United States of America—the "melting pot" of cultures, after all.

When the ceremony began, the intensity, the meaning, and the gravity of the situation dawned on me. It all felt too real, too vulnerable. I felt like the walls were closing in on me, singling me out and calling out my emotions. Looking at the crowd around me was like looking in a mirror; in that moment, they were just like me. I did not know why, but something about the ceremony was emotionally overwhelming. When the time came for us to stand up and say the oath, an intense flash of vulnerability overcame me. I felt bare, naked standing in that ceremony room with all of those people, so vulnerable that I felt almost embarrassed. It sounds impossible and cliché, but I swear I felt my heart and soul connect with everyone around me. I felt ridiculous. I came into this ceremony with low expectations and not a care in the world, and there I was, a puddle of emotions and vulnerability. A potent sense of pride and happiness washed over me, and it felt as if those around me could also see into my heart. I was happy, but I felt exposed, as if everyone could get into my head and hear all my thoughts.

At the end of the ceremony, they announced that there were fifty-two different countries represented that Saturday morning. Fifty-two. All of these people from all around the world understood me. They held onto their original country yet also embraced America. We all stood there together—vulnerable, but overall and most importantly, proud.

Chapter 12

Rise Up

Ratatouille

If America is a melting pot
then let me add my own spice,
my own flavor
like basil leaves or paprika.

Don't Write A Boring Song

A piece of music consists of many notes.
Would anyone want to listen to a song
with only one?
A one-note song would be boring,
wrong, weird,
could not exist.

Life Advice

no one likes a racist
when it comes to
your own self.

Chapter 13

Know Your Worth

———

Evolution

Three years old
an eager child—
shiny-eyed, bright, optimistic—
charged into the world
with open arms.

Seven years old,
energetic and sporadic
learning the world's wonders
untouched by bias and hate.

Thirteen years old,
learning about the world
as it is painted over
in dark red, brown,
and countless other colors.

Seventeen years old,
anxious and sometimes hate-filled
and angry at the world for its crimes
against me and the ones I love.

Twenty years old,
accepting the shades of the world,
even the dark and hateful ones,
once again eager and shiny-eyed.

Rise

Fire, fire, fire,
something everyone has,
despite any negativity you see in yourself.

Whether you grew up thinking you were
lesser than or submissive,
You will always have the fire, fire, fire.

You are more than a stereotype—
mark my words. You are any and everything
you want yourself to be.

Protection, Resilience, Desire, Passion
we fight, and in our struggle,
we rise.

I Am More Than Yellow

Yellow
The color of my skin—
at least that's what people say it is.
Based on this color, people make
many assumptions, as if
this color supposedly reveals
a lot about me to others.

Pink
Sensitivity, vulnerability, love.
The fleeting moments of weakness,
the warmth creeping up my cheeks
and flushing them red,
the roller-coaster butterflies
threatening to burst from my stomach.

Black
Strength of character overcomes,
helps you to fight for yourself.
Loving yourself, you stand armed
guns ready to fire
for a fight that is relentless,
where you never give up.

Red
A fiery passion burns deep
in the depths of your soul,
a desire to achieve, learn, motivate.
Resilience is second nature,
propelling you into the future,

ready to take it all.

Scattered Soul

I rejoice in the fact that
    different shards of
        my heart and soul
    are scattered throughout different
        crevices of the world,
            in different nooks and crannies.

    For exploring the world's treasures
        through meeting new people
    different from me,
        allows me to learn little by little
        about different parts of the world.
    each new person that I encounter,
        I hope they bring a part of
    me back to their world.

    Doesn't traveling the world
through others sound intoxicating?
    Learning about different
foods, traditions, clothing, music,
people sharing their stories with each other,
    and spreading culture and backgrounds,
sounds so riveting.

The Magician in the Garden

A secret garden, dark and mysterious,
yet filled with sunshine and warmth,
dripping with beauty that makes others envious.
treasures of the world, full of charm.

Magical and exuberant this garden can be,
you have this specially in you.
So do not let the pests eat away at your trees,
don't let your foes make you blue.

And if the pests try to bring you down,
keep your roots, remember who you are.
Look inside your heart, do not frown,
and see the unique garden you are.

The pests, they can be taken away
but the garden can never be,
for the true you cannot be cast astray,
don't let your garden fill with debris.

Pests come and go, they are never long-term,
don't let your magic be for naught.
For sometimes we must shield ourselves from storms—
hurricanes, tornadoes and drought.

This secret garden has magic, that's clear,
that no mighty storm can bring down.
Ruler of the magic, look in the mirror,
you will see you are wearing a crown.

Dig Your Toes into the Earth

Carve your initials
into this earth
and stand your ground.

Defiled, violated—
despite that, rise
and fight.

Swing from branch to branch
climb the tree on the left
and the tree on the right.

Dare to look into the honeycomb
even if there are bees
because the honey is worth it.

Plant every seed
water every plant
cut down the ones you don't like.

But never ever hold back,
ever hold back,
if what you feel in your soul

beckons you to pursue it.
Break out of the cage,
the mold!

He can do it?
So can you!

Swing from branch to branch

and plant every seed.
For that is truly living life
and allowing yourself to be you.

Mother Nature

Mother Earth gives you a love
that may sometimes be tough,
do not spit it back into her face
for she is kind and patient
but you, too, must be kind
to yourself.

Mother Nature gives you a home.
Do not hide away, don't let the others decide.
You are given your own life—
opportunity, personality—
why spend your days hiding
in the shadows of the unworthy?

To violate your own rights
is the ultimate insult
to the earth on which we reside,
but also to yourself.
Violated, broken, hurt
yet still standing tall.

With the strength of a thousand iron horses
no man or woman can bring
you down to your knees.
No, never bow down to your knees.
It is the ultimate self-betrayal
when a person cannot grasp their own worth.

Silent Cosmic Power

She wears a bulletproof vest
but doesn't carry a gun.
Kindness everlasting,
radiant with warmth,

forgiving and relenting,
yielding to the world,
causing some to judge
her perceived weakness.

She seems to not fight for herself
but she does, she does every day,
just in her own way, for in her mind
she knows the strength

that threatens to burst
from her lungs and
the crevices of her body, that is
a power unmatched, almost cosmic.

A power that does not need to be flaunted
for it is this power
that is so strong
it needs no outside validation.

This power is essential
to support, love, and nurture
the darkness of the world
into something a little brighter.

Treasure Trove

My stomach holds a treasure trove
of words
and ideals
and tastes
that you do not know about

But worry not
you can reach into the mystery
and see for yourself
That you and I are
one and the same

Despite the color of my shell
and the smell of my hair
or the size of my nose
don't be scared of difference
celebrate it instead

For if we mix the
different treasure troves
that we hold so dear inside
Something so beautiful can blossom
something new, something real.

Sugar, Spice, and Everything Yummy

A delicious meal
consists of different flavors—
that is the key to good cooking.
If you only use salt
no sugar, no spice, no other flavor
the meal will be bland.

Equality Is Very Important

Walk the earth as an equal to others
yield your worth to no one else.

Chapter 14

Resolution

NGUYỄN ĐAN THY AND TEE WIN

AGE TWELVE

In front of me, a rustic chestnut door awaits. As I make my way toward the familiar door, obstacles scatter the path; I dodge, jump over, and skirt past them. I push the door handle once, twice, three times. It opens and I peek inside. Tentatively, I step inside, but the door refuses to open further. I can see everything in the room so clearly, every nook and cranny, but am unable to enter.

I am Vietnamese.

I grew up in Saigon, Vietnam, but moved to the United States at age twelve. Before I moved to America, in Vietnam, the way I spoke and acted set me apart from the local people. People often said to me, "Say that again; you sound funny when you say that word." Waiters at restaurants or family friends often asked me to repeat what I said because my Vietnamese accent was not good enough. My Vietnamese accent was and is not authentic enough. This is due to the fact that all my life, I was educated in Saigon's international schools. I spent the bulk of my day speaking in English, working in English, and thinking in English. Because of this, English became a sort of native tongue for me.

Even as a supposed native Vietnamese person, I drifted away from my Vietnamese roots. Because I used English the most, I subconsciously mixed it into my Vietnamese. Language is the basis of an identity, so I wonder: if you don't speak a language near-perfectly, can you truly claim its identity? I feel like the language barrier is always going to separate me from being "purely Vietnamese." I *am* still fluent in my native language, despite my inauthentic pronunciation. I understand the slang and cultural references. I am able to communicate with others . . . for the most part.

I am not Vietnamese.

AGE FOURTEEN

Defeated, I turn behind me. Another door awaits: a large glass double door. Again, I try to enter. A different set of obstacles blocks my way. Crash. Attempt to enter #42,902: failure. I'm back to square one.

I am American.

Here in Houston, Texas, I generally fit in. My friends are loving and always there for me, and I have developed a strong circle of support. I like the food here, I like the roads, I like the malls, I like it all. However, there are moments where I do feel a bit like an outsider.

Here, I have been labelled with every stereotype one could imagine: My English is impressive. Yes, I am related to your one Asian acquaintance. I know karate but I'm not good at sports. I will marry an Asian. Of course I can help you with your math homework; I'm Chinese. My family owns a nail salon, and we eat dogs. I am equally an outsider here. I feel fairly comfortable in this culture of immigrants, each of us sharing a common sense of alienation, yet I'm still grasping at a sense of belonging. I have to admit, I don't care too much for the Super Bowl or Groundhog Day or backyard barbecues. I find myself missing Vietnam's Moon Festival and Tết celebrations. I thought I would eventually fit in, but years later, I'm still stuck on the periphery.

I am not American.

AGE SEVENTEEN
I live in the hallway between the two doors, open to both but belonging in neither.

I feel as if I am in a perpetual cultural purgatory. When I spend summers in my birthplace of Saigon, I am not recognized as "native Vietnamese." Yet I am also not "American enough" to avoid the stupid comments from clerks at drug stores and the occasional ignorant classmate. I've heard it all: "Wait, what? You got a D on that test? You're Asian, I thought y'all were supposed to be good at math." In Saigon, the comments are slightly different, but still the same: "Take that dish to the American (me) sitting at the table in the corner." "You actually understood that reference?"

I've spent a long time trying to belong somewhere, clinging to whatever connection I felt with a country, unwilling to embrace my true identity. A true identity, I used to believe, only existed with a sense of belonging to a specific place. I was wrong. An identity is the reality of a person's experiences. Everyone has an identity unique to them.

Some claim the "Vietnamese" identity while others claim "American." Some claim neither.

AGE TWENTY
I belong in both doors, able to slide in and out of both.

When people ask me where I'm from, I tell them, "I was born in Vietnam and moved here during middle school. So, I'm kind of a bit of both—I'm from Vietnam and from Houston." I am proud that I have a dual sense of identity. I embrace the fact that there is difference and diversity in me. It did not feel right for me to say that I was just Vietnamese, or just American, or from nowhere. It is the exact opposite—I feel a connection with both places that is so strong, I consider myself to be from both.

I love the fact that I have best friends in both the United States and Vietnam. To me, friends and family are what make a home, home. I have found my people in both places and I could not be happier.

I am both Nguyễn Đan Thy and Tee Win, Vietnamese and American, comfortable opening any door.

www.ingramcontent.com/pod-product-compliance
Lightning Source LLC
LaVergne TN
LVHW011846060526
838200LV00054B/4193